SAINTS IN EVANGELISM
STUDY GUIDE
BY J JOHN
& MICHAEL MITTON

Saints in
Evangelism

A course in friendship evangelism

Study Guide

J John

LYNX
COMMUNICATIONS

Anglican
Renewal
Ministries

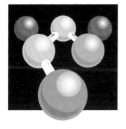

INTRODUCTION

WELCOME TO SAINTS IN EVANGELISM!

This Study Guide is for use with the *Saints in Evangelism* Video, and provides you with:

- A brief summary of the teaching which is given on the video
- Notes for group leaders
- Exercises
- Daily studies.

THE COURSE FOR GROUPS

Many people will be doing the course as part of a small group, and this is probably the best way of learning for this course. Church leaders will need to appoint a group leader (or leaders) for the course. The group leader is responsible for leading each session, arranging for the video to be played (making sure it is cued in the right place etc), guiding the group through the exercises, and helping each member of the group to feel at home. Each session contains notes to guide group leaders.

Groups should not be bigger than twelve, and they will need to be in a room where everyone can see a TV screen. Each person will need to have a Study Guide, a pen, some paper and a Bible.

THE COURSE FOR FAMILIES

It may be that you have bought the Video and the Study Guide and you would like to do the course as a family – parents, children, grandparents, and maybe one or two 'extended family' members. With family and close friends, you could probably soon find yourself with about a dozen in a group.

Make sure you know who is going to be group leader (you might want to share the leadership around), and each person will need a Study Guide, a pen, some paper and a Bible. Make sure everyone can see the TV Screen. Children will probably want to be over twelve years of age if they are to really enjoy this course.

THE COURSE FOR INDIVIDUALS

You might want to take the Video and Study Guide home and do this course on your own as a kind of 'DIY Evangelism Training Kit'. It will work perfectly well like this. Where necessary we have adjusted the exercises to suit an individual rather than a group approach.

THE VIDEO   Check that your video recorder is in good working order, and before each meeting make sure you have the video correctly cued. Each Video session lasts about half an hour and usually there are two or three breaks during this for exercises.

EXERCISES   In the Study Guide we have expanded some of the exercises, so you will find some variation from the exercises which J John sets on the Video. Where there is variation, we suggest you follow this Study Guide rather than the Video.

HOMEWORK   On the video J John sets homework to do each week. You will find this recorded at the start of the Daily Study section.

SUMMARY NOTES   For each session in this Study Guide you will find notes summarizing the teaching on the Video. We suggest you don't try and follow these notes while watching the Video, but use them as a resource afterwards.

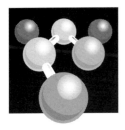

SESSION 1
Why evangelise?

WHY WE DON'T EVANGELISE

The founder of the Church Army, Wilson Carlile, once said:

Anglicans are like Arctic rivers: frozen at the mouth.

There are many fears that prevent us from sharing our faith with others. Some of them are:

Fear of being inadequate

Rather than being concerned about what we do **not** know, we should share what we **do** know. Jesus taught profound truths in simple ways. We should feel quite free to say, 'I don't know' to people's questions, but at the same time, when we do come across questions that we don't know the answer to, we should go and do some homework.

Fear of losing our reputation

We are so often concerned about what others will think of us. Jesus' example is summed up in Philippians:

Phil 2:7   *…he made himself nothing.*

If we are to be serious about evangelising, we must be prepared to look foolish.

Fear of rejection

Luke 4:29   Right at the start of his ministry, Jesus experienced rejection . The Greek word for **witness** is 'marturia' from which we derive the English word, 'martyr'. As Paul makes clear to his good friend Timothy:

everyone who wants to live a godly life in Christ Jesus will be
2 Tim 3:12   *persecuted.*

We need to own up to these fears, and confess them. Like the disciples in Acts 4:29–31, we should learn to pray for boldness.

WHAT IS EVANGELISM?

CH Spurgeon said:

Evangelism is one beggar telling another beggar where to find bread.

The Anglican Archbishops Consultation in Cyprus in 1989 resolved:

To evangelise is to make known by word and deed the love of the crucified and risen Christ in the power of the Holy Spirit, so that people will repent, believe and receive Christ as their Saviour and obediently serve him as their Lord in the fellowship of his Church.

In the New Testament, the verb 'to evangelise' is used 52 times. Its meaning is to declare, proclaim, announce or state Good News. Jesus' ministry was to evangelise, as summed up in Luke 4:18. It is clear from this and from the life and ministry of Jesus that the proclamation of the Good News is one side of the coin (words), and that the demonstration of the Good News (works and wonders) is the other.

WHY SHOULD WE EVANGELISE?

Because the Bible commands it

In Matthew, Jesus gives the Great Commission. We see three things in this passage:

- **Make** disciples   – *bring to commitment to Christ*
- **Mark** disciples   – *baptism*
- **Mature** disciples – *teaching*

Matthew 28:19–20

Because of people's needs

If we really love God, we will love people. Jesus evangelised because of the depth of compassion in his heart for people who were like sheep without a shepherd.

Matthew 9:36–38

Because Jesus believed in evangelism

Jesus was committed to the growth of his church:

Wherever he went he proclaimed the Good News of the Kingdom of God and backed up his preaching with demonstrations of the power and love of God.

Mark 1:32–34

Because the early church believed in evangelism

As you will see from Exercise Three, it is clear that the first Christians believed in growth. The church in Jerusalem grew from 120 to many thousands.

Acts 21:20

Because the fulfilment of prophecy demands evangelism

Jesus said:

The gospel of the Kingdom will be preached in the whole world as a testimony to all nations, and then the end will come.

Matthew 24:14

The world population at the time of Jesus was about 170 million. In 1992 the world population has been estimated at around 5,420 million. There are 218 nations – all must hear the Good News!

Because the majority of churches believe this should be a Decade of Evangelism

Resolution 43 of the 1988
Lambeth Conference

This conference, recognising that evangelism is the primary task given to the Church, asks each Province and Diocese of the Anglican Communion, in co-operation with other Christians, to make the closing years of this millennium a Decade of Evangelism with a renewed and united emphasis on making Christ known to the people of this world.

■ VIDEO EXERCISE ■

During the session we shall look at church growth in the book of Acts. It will be helpful to have the guide open, ready to record the numbers required. You won't find precise numbers by all of these, but there may be references that indicate growth (eg: *the number of disciples was increased*).

1:15 _group numbered about 120_

2:41 _____

2:47 _____

4:4 _____

5:14 _____

6:1 _____

6:7 _____

21:20 _____ (approx 25 years later)

Group Leaders

As this is the first meeting of the group, give time to introduce each other. Ask each person what their hopes are as they approach this course. They may find it helpful to express their fears as well. During the next six weeks, this group is going to learn much and travel a long way together, so spend some moments in prayer together, committing this important journey to the Lord. Invite the Holy Spirit to come and work in each member of the group, that by the end of the course each person will be equipped and enthused to spread the Good News of Jesus to their friends and neighbours.

Take a look through the exercises before the meeting and work out how long you want to spend on each one. Please note that Exercise One involves ministry. If you prefer, you might like to leave this until near the end of the evening where you can give yourself time to pray and minister to one another.

Check that each person has a Study Guide and that they understand how to use the Daily Studies. Make sure each person has a Bible – they will need one for each session.

EXERCISE ONE

What are your fears as you consider evangelising your friends? Imagine I have just asked you to go to your neighbour with the express intention of telling them about Jesus! If the thought of this causes fear to rise up, what is the fear about?

Spend some time confessing these fears to the Lord.

For some people, these fears may be very deep rooted, and you may find it helpful to seek a friend who can pray with you for inner healing outside of this meeting.

Now pray for the Holy Spirit to come and heal you, and give you boldness. If you are part of a group, minister to one another. Don't hurry this bit – it may be that God wants to move deeply and powerfully among you. If necessary, you can do the rest of the session's work at another time.

EXERCISE TWO

Write down two or three definitions of evangelism.

1 _____
2 _____
3 _____
4 _____

For those in groups, discuss these together.

EXERCISE THREE

What reasons can you give for why we should evangelise.

1 _____
2 _____
3 _____
4 _____

For those in groups talk about these together

DAILY STUDY

DAILY STUDY

Luke 15:8–32

The following readings are for your personal use during the week prior to the next session. Try and give a little time every day to each reading. Also, go back over these notes. Particularly spend time thinking about the list of reasons for evangelism (both mine and yours) and familiarise yourself with them.

DAY°ONE

Read Luke 15:3–7.

This passage shows the priority of evangelism. The shepherd is willing to risk 99 sheep to reach the lost one. We cannot just hope that the lost one will come back to the fold, we must leave the fold and go out to the lost one. From the parable of the Lost Sheep to the parables of the Lost Coin and the Lost Son, it's as though Jesus is trying to reinforce his point. Every lost person matters to God.

Pause and reflect on the parable of the Lost Sheep.
Do you know people who used to be Christians but are no longer committed? Pray for them.
Ask the Lord to show you if you should do anything.

Prayer

Lord, look through my eyes
Listen through my ears
Speak through my lips
Act with my hands
Walk with my feet… Amen

DAY TWO

Read Mark 4:30–32.

Jesus predicted the growth of his Kingdom from a small beginning. It is good to notice how this prediction has been proven true over the last 2,000 years.
Look back at the growth of the Church in the Book of Acts, and be encouraged that it continues to grow.
Spend a few moments praising and thanking the Lord that his Word is bearing fruit, and then praying for the continued growth of the Church.

Prayer

O Lord Christ, who called your disciples not only to follow you, but to become fishers of mankind, give to us and to your whole Church grace to obey your word. Grant that, attempting great things for you, we may also expect great things from you; to whom be glory for ever and ever… Amen

DAY THREE

Read Matthew 9:35–38.

Notice the word **harassed** in v36; this word in the Greek means to be 'whipped and beaten'. There are many today burdened with fears, anxieties and guilt.

Now notice the word 'compassion' in the same verse. Jim Wallis in his book *A Call to Conversion* writes:

A very wise old man once told me the difference between concern and compassion. Being concerned is seeing something awful happening and feeling, hey, that's really too bad. Having compassion, he said, is seeing the same thing and saying, 'I just can't let that happen', and obviously trying to do something about it.

Thought

No one person can change the world. But we can change the world for one person.

Prayer

Ask God to lay on your heart people and situations for which you can intercede:

Lord, teach me to pray, to want to pray, to delight to pray. When I pray, teach me to pray with faith, with hope, with love. Let me make prayer my first work, my persistent work, my most important work. Let my prayer be a channel for your love, your peace, for those for whom I pray, and for myself. O dear and blessed Lord... Amen.

Eric Milner White

DAY FOUR

Read again Matthew 9:35–38.

Reflect on Jesus' comment in v37 and his encouragement to pray for more labourers in v38. Make a list of all those you know who are employed in missionary work. If you do not know of anyone, pray for me.

1 *J John*	6
2	7
3	8
4	9
5	10

Reflect

2 Thessalonians 3:1
(Jerusalem Bible)

Pray for us; pray that the Lord's message may spread quickly, and be received with honour as it was among you and pray that we may be preserved from the interference of bigoted evil people.

Pray for those listed and then pray for more labourers to go out into the harvest field. Pray for some from your church to be called.

DAY FIVE

Read 1 Corinthians 12:12–31.

The most used term in the Bible for the Church is 'the Body of Christ'. The Church is a body, not a business; that means the Church is alive. All living things grow.

Spend some time praying for the leaders and staff of your Church. Write their names and pray for God's grace, wisdom and protection to be given to them.

1 _____   6 _____
2 _____   7 _____
3 _____   8 _____
4 _____   9 _____
5 _____   10 _____

Pray for the growth of the Church.

Prayer

Simeon took the baby Jesus in his arms and praised God saying:

Sovereign Lord, as you have promised,
you now dismiss your servant in peace.
For my eyes have seen your salvation,
Luke 2: 29–32   *which you have prepared in the sight of all people.*

Read again 1 Corinthians 12:12–31.

None of us have got it together, but together we have got it. Each part has a part.
Spend some time praying about what your part is in furthering God's Kingdom.
Write down what you are currently doing for him.
What do you sense the Spirit of God is guiding you to do?
Spend some time praying about what you have written. Ask the Lord for confirmation and wisdom to know the next step.

Prayer

Christ has no body now on earth but yours, no hands but yours, no feet but yours. Yours are the eyes through which you must look out with Christ's compassion on the world. Yours are the feet with which he is to go about doing good. Yours are the hands with which he blesses
St Teresa of Avila   *now… Amen.*

DAY SIX

1 Corinthians 9:22

Read 1 Corinthians 9:19–23. Notice this verse:

...so that by all possible means I might save some.

Courses and books on evangelism are only useful if they help us to be effective witnesses to the Good News. If all they do is pass on interesting information or fuel discussions, then the courses have failed.

Spend some time praying for this course. Pray for each person in the group. Pray for the Spirit's illumination to help us to think it through. Pray for wisdom to know what needs to be applied personally and what needs to be done corporately, by the body of the Church.

Pray for God's Holy Spirit to inspire us with the same urgency and passion that the Apostle Paul had in today's reading.

Prayer

Take, Lord, all my liberty, my memory, my understanding and my whole will. You have given me all that I have, all that I am, and I surrender all to your divine will, that you dispose of me. Give me only your love and your grace. With this I am rich enough, and have no more to ask... Amen.

Ignatius of Loyola

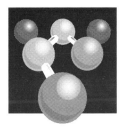

SESSION 2
What is the Good News that we share?

THE GOOD NEWS DIAGRAM

During this session you will learn to explain the Good News clearly through a diagram which can be used whenever the opportunity arises. The diagram is based on the stories in the early chapters of Genesis. Don't spend time worrying about whether or not Adam and Eve actually existed. The important thing for this session is to learn about the truths expressed in these chapters.

God

In the beginning, before there was anything else was God.

GOD

God made the world

Genesis 1:1–2 · *In the beginning God created the heavens and the earth*

See Genesis 1 for how he made the world.

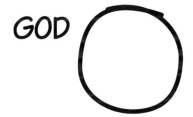

Evil enters the world

Colossians 1:16

Satan was created by God, and originally he was good. But with his free will he chose to rebel, and Genesis 3 gives the story of Satan's influence over the world. Jesus referred to Satan as the

John 14:30 *prince of this world* and the apostle John wrote:

1 John 5:19 *The world is under the control of the evil one.*

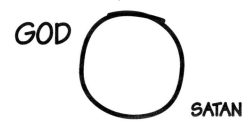

The tree of life

Genesis 2:9

In the garden of Eden God planted two trees, the first of which was the tree of life. This represents all the good things of God.

The tree of knowledge of good and evil

Genesis 2:16–17

The other tree in the garden was the tree of knowledge of good and evil. This represents the choice we have to make: either good or evil. To choose evil means death.

Man and woman

Genesis 1:26–28

Man and woman are created to enjoy the gift of life, but with the ability to choose either good or evil.

Satan's influence

Satan tempted Adam and Eve to eat of the tree of the knowledge of good and evil. He tempted them to disobey God, and like Satan, they rebelled. As a result they were cut off from God and the tree of life.

Genesis 3:1–7

Genesis 3:21–24

The Cross of Jesus – God's rescue act

The word the Bible uses for **rescue** is 'redeem'. The Cross is God reaching out to rescue us and unite separated parties. St Paul wrote:

Ephesians 1:7 *In Christ we have redemption through his blood*

Accepting Christ

We therefore can come to God through Jesus.
We **admit** that we have been deceived by Satan and have sinned.
We **commit** our lives to God.
We **submit** our lives to the teaching of Jesus.
We **transmit** the message of Jesus to a world longing to hear the Good News.

EXERCISE

EXERCISE

For group leaders

Before the meeting gets underway, check how people found the Daily Studies. Have they done them? Now is the time to find out! Ask the group if, between them, they can remember the reasons for evangelism that we discussed in Session 1.

Make sure each member of the group has a sheet of paper and a pen for Exercise Two. I suggest you become very familiar with the diagram yourself, so that you can easily help the others to learn. Remember, for some people this kind of thing brings back all sorts of schoolday fears of failure – assure them it is not an exam!

Prepare the evening carefully, and if you have got someone who can lead worship, get in touch with them to see if they could lead some songs of praise at the end of the evening.

EXERCISE ONE

In twos or threes, ask each other, 'what is a Christian?' Remember, you are not trying to attempt a long explanation, but just a few words in a couple of sentences.

Once you have had your say, then in the small groups of two or three talk together about your answers.

- Would they be helpful to an unbeliever?
- Did you use jargon? – be honest!!

If you are on your own, write down your answer and have a think about it.

EXERCISE TWO

Before you do this exercise, are you sure you have understood all the parts to the diagram? Don't be afraid to ask, because we are all learning.

Get into pairs and see if you can use the diagram to explain the Good News. Try and do it without looking at the diagram in this book, but if you need to have a look then do so. Don't take too long over it, and please remember you are not sitting an exam! The main idea is just to get a feel of it, so that you can begin to learn how to use it. Make sure you both have time to do the diagram.

If you are on your own, write out the diagram, making sure you understand each section of it. If you are not clear, rewind the video and watch it again.

When everyone has finished doing the exercises, come back together again as a group and talk about what you have learned from the diagram. Is there anything new you have discovered about the Good News?

DAILY STUDY

DAILY STUDY

As part of your studies this week, famliarize yourself with the diagram. To get it into your head, draw it out at every opportunity! Better still, try it out on a friend who is not a Christian. They may have been wanting someone to explain the gospel to them for years.

DAY ONE

I believe in God, the Father Almighty, Maker of heaven and earth.

Please read Acts 17:16–29

Jesus addressed God as **Abba**, an Aramaic word which means 'Daddy'.

Mark 14:36

"Abba, Father," he said, "everything is possible for you. Take this cup from me. Yet not what I will, but what you will."

So when Jesus called God 'Abba', he was expressing his own intimate relationship with God. It is also found in Romans:

Romans 8:15

For you did not receive a Spirit that makes you a slave again to fear, but you received the Spirit of sonship. And by him we cry 'Abba Father'

And in Galatians:

Galatians 4:6

Because you are sons, God sent the Spirit of his Son into our hearts, the Spirit who calls out 'Abba Father'.

Jesus first applied the term 'Abba Father' to God and gave authority to his disciples to do so. And the Apostle Paul sees in its use a symbol of the Christian's adoption as a child of God and their possession of the Spirit.

Many people today have a bad father image because of their human parent model. Pray that we may afresh know, trust and experience God as our Father. And pray that he may bring his healing to those who have a marred perception of him.

Prayer

Father, I abandon myself into your hands; do with me what you will. Whatever you may do, I thank you; I am ready for all, I accept all. Let your will be done in me. I wish no more than this, O Lord. Into your hands I commend my soul; I offer it to you with all the love of my heart. For I love you, Lord, and so wish to give myself, to surrender myself into your hands without reserve and with boundless confidence for you are my Father... Amen

The Apostles Creed

I believe in Jesus Christ, his only Son, our Lord, who was conceived by the Holy Spirit, born of the virgin Mary.

Read Matthew 1:18 to 2:12.

Messiah is a Hebrew word which means 'Anointed One'. In the Greek language it is translated as 'Christos' – Christ.

The Nicene Creed continues and says of Jesus that he is:

The Nicene Creed

God from God, light from light, true God from true God, begotten, not made, one in being with the Father.

All these words have been calculated to emphasise that in Jesus it is the God of Creation who meets us and saves us. In Jesus we see and experience God.

The Latin word for Lord, **dominus**, means 'one who owns slaves'. In other words, your Lord is someone who has ownership over you. When we call Jesus 'Lord', we acknowledge and profess that Jesus is the One who owns our loyalty.

This idea may seem unreal for us today. But in the early church, Caesar worship was the official religion of the Roman Empire. Once every year all citizens of the Empire had to appear before the magistrates in order to burn a pinch of incense to the godhead of Caesar while saying 'Caesar is Lord'. But Jesus Christ alone is Lord and many Christians, refusing to deny that fact, submitted to persecution, imprisonment and martyrdom.

Anonymous

If he is not Lord of all, he is not Lord at all.

Pray that we will not only know God as Father, but also as Lord and have a sense of awe, respect and humility.

Pray that he may be Lord of all in the church and that inconsistencies in our own life and church may be put right.

Prayer

The Jesus Prayer of the Orthodox Church

Lord Jesus Christ, Son of God,
have mercy on me, a sinner.

The Apostles' Creed

He suffered under Pontius Pilate, was crucified, dead and buried. He descended to the dead.

Read John 18:28 to 19:22.

The word **atonement** means 'the bringing together of two estranged and separated parties'. Sin originated when we turned our back on God. We were created in God's likeness to live in the world and to enjoy an intimate relationship with him. Because God is love, we were not forced into this relationship; we were given the free will to choose, to accept or to reject God. But we have turned away from God. This had the immediate effect of cutting us off from him.

The basic meaning of the life, death and resurrection of Jesus is that:

2 Corinthians 5:19 *God was reconciling the world to himself in Christ.*

Jesus died so that we, living or dying, might be truly at one with God because of Christ's forgiveness, so that nothing in all creation, not even death itself, will ever again separate us from God's presence.

Romans 8:31–39

If Jesus Christ were to come today, people would not crucify him. They would ask him to dinner and hear what he had to say and then make fun of him.

Thomas Carlyle

Let us reflect and thank Jesus for all the suffering he went through to enable us to be part of the family of God. This is the key that many people need to find truth and life.

Prayer

Teach us good Lord, to serve you as you deserve,
to give and not to count the cost,
to fight and not to heed the wounds,
to toil and not to seek for rest,
to labour and not to ask for any reward
save that of knowing that we do your will... Amen.

St Ignatius

DAY FOUR

The Apostles' Creed *The third day he rose again from the dead.*

Read John 20:1–29.

In many churches on Easter Sunday, the minister will say, **'Christ is risen'** and the congregation respond **'He is risen indeed'**.

The resurrection of Jesus Christ from the dead is the foundation of Christianity; if he did not rise from the dead, then there is no truth in Christianity, it does not have anything to stand on. Christianity as a religion is unique because it is based on the death and resurrection of its founder. So either it is the biggest hoax in the history of the world or it is true.

Without the resurrection, the Christian movement would have petered out in ignominy and there would have been no Christianity. It is not too much to say that without the resurrection the phenomenon of Christianity in the apostolic age and since is scientifically unaccountable. It is also true to say that without the resurrection Christianity would not be itself, as the distinctiveness of Christianity is not its adherence to a teacher who lived long ago, but in its belief that 'Jesus is Lord' for every generation through the centuries.

Michael Ramsey – former
Archbishop of Canterbury

Let us pray that we will know the resurrected Jesus in a new way today. Pray that our experience of him may be similar to that of the two disciples whom he met on the road to Emmaus.

Luke 24:32 *Were not our hearts burning within us while he talked with us on the road and opened the Scriptures to us?*

Prayer

You are the light of minds that know you; the life of souls that love you; and the strength of wills that serve you.

Help us to know you so that we may truly love you; help us to love you so that we may fully serve you, because in serving you we find perfect
Augustine *freedom… Amen*

DAY FIVE

Apostles' Creed *He ascended into heaven and is seated at the right hand of the Father.*

Read Acts 1:6–11.

Acts 1:3 The word **ascension** is used to describe the departure of Jesus from the earth. Ascension Day is celebrated 40 days after Easter. Jesus Christ returned to his Father and so to the place of power and authority.

The ascension shows that Jesus:

Hebrews 9 :24–26 • has completed his redeeming work on earth

John 14:2 • has gone ahead to prepare a place for his followers

Hebrews 7:25
Romans 8:34 • prays for us

Hebrews 1:3 • rules with his Father

1 Corinthians 15:24 • is waiting to return to establish the Kingdom of God.

What wonderful truths and thoughts for us while we wait and persevere in his service. Pray today that these truths will inspire us to 'good works'.

Prayer

Lord, grant me the grace of a deep, fervent and living faith in you and all that you have revealed.

Take away all pride, vanity, insincerity, self-interest, and anything that may hinder me from accepting your truth.

Help me to trust in you and have strength and wholeness. Lead me and guide me so that I may grow in your love and holiness… Amen.

The Apostles' Creed

He will come to judge the living and the dead and his Kingdom will have no end.

Read 2 Peter 3:1–13.

Three devils were talking and trying to decide how they could keep Christians from being effective. One devil said...

I know, let's tell Christians that there is no heaven. No possibility of rewards. That will keep them quiet.

Another devil said...

No, let's just tell them there is no hell. No possibility of punishment. That will keep them quiet.

And the third devil said...

No, wait a minute. I've got it! Let's not tell them there's no heaven or that there's no hell. Let's just tell them there's plenty of time, there's no hurry.

There is so little time and so much to do. So let us labour in the vineyard.

Once a man is united to God, how could he not live forever? Once a man is separated from God, what can he do but wither and die?

C S Lewis

So we must:

Matthew 24:42 • watch

Matthew 24:44 • be ready

1 Corinthians 9:24–25 • guard our own spiritual lives

1 Peter 4:10 • live faithfully

Luke 19:10, John 20:21 • pray and work to 'seek and save the lost' (what this course is all about).

Prayer

Bestow on me, O Lord my God, an understanding that knows you, wisdom in finding you, a way of life that is pleasing to you, perseverance that faithfully waits for you and confidence that I may meet you at the end... Amen.

Thomas Aquinas

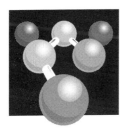

SESSION 3
What is friendship evangelism?

JERUSALEM, JUDEA AND BEYOND

The evangelistic strategy given to us by Jesus is recorded in the opening chapter of Acts where Jesus said:

You will receive power when the Holy Spirit comes on you and you will be my witnesses in Jerusalem and in all Judea and Samaria and to the ends of the earth.

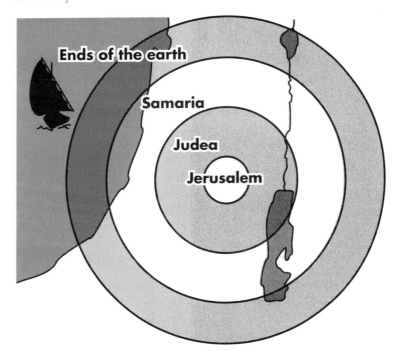

Starting in Jerusalem

Why does Jesus tell them to start in Jerusalem? Because it was where they were. We should start evangelising where we are. Our Jerusalem is our home and our immediate circle of family and friends, neighbours etc. Jerusalem is also the place of the disciples' failure. God might well call us to share our faith with those amongst whom we feel we have failed. Where we have failed to share Christ with our close family and friends, we should start by saying…

I'm sorry – I'm sorry I have never shared with you the thing that is most important to me.

Acts 20:20 In the Acts of the Apostles, the gospel went 'from house to house'. So the gospel goes from our home to the homes of others we already know. There are three natural access areas:

- Kinship (family and close friends).
- Community (people we regularly meet with, eg: milkman, window-cleaner, newsagent, neighbours).
- Common Interest (share same meeting place; eg: squash club, darts team, night class etc.).

We particularly concentrate on 'Jerusalem' in this course, because this is where friendship evangelism takes place. Once we are effective in evangelism in Jerusalem, we can start moving out.

Judea represents the evangelism of those friends and contacts we don't see so regularly.

Samaria they were enemies of the Jews, so this represents the evangelism of those we don't get on with. You may not like them, and they may not like you, but at least you have a relationship with them, even if it is a bad one!

The ends of the earth this represents the evangelism of those we do not know, through missions, door to door etc.

WHY PEOPLE COME TO CHURCH

Here are some statistics, I have come across, about what attracted people into coming to church:

- 1% said they came because they were visited by church members (this figure can vary considerably).
- 2% said they came because of a special church programme (eg: a children's holiday club).
- 3% came because of a special need (eg: bereavement).
- 3% came because of Sunday School.
- 6% came because of publicity (note: this is a high figure).
- 8% came because of personal contact with the minister or church staff.
- 77% came because they were invited by Christian friends and relatives.

What can we do?

- Start loving people through prayer.
- Where we think we have failed, apologise.
- Sow the seed of the gospel generously but sensitively on an 'as need' basis.
- Expect people to be interested. Have a listening ear to where they are at. Don't be afraid to ask them what they believe.
- Make use of Christian tapes and books.
- Invite them to a suitable meeting or service.

EXERCISE

EXERCISE

For group leaders

Before you start the video, find out how people have progressed with the Daily Studies. Have they got the hang of the diagram? Has anyone used it during the week with an unbeliever?

There are three exercises for this session. The first and third involve a Bible study – make sure everyone has a Bible in hand. Remember, if there are young Christians in the group, you may need to help them find the references.

The second exercise is very important, so make sure you give plenty of time to it.

EXERCISE ONE

In the New Testament, the Good News was often spread through existing relationships. Look up the following passages, and fill in the blanks (you can find the answers in small type at the end of this Session if you need them).

John 1:41   1   Andrew brought _____

John 1:43–45   2   Philip told _____

              (Notice Philip, Andrew and Peter were all from the same area)

John 4:28–30   3   The Samaritan woman told _____

Luke 5:27–32   4   Levi invited his _____

Acts 16:25–34   5   The Philippian jailer shared with _____

Now fill in the missing words:

Day after day, in the temple courts and _____

_____

Acts 5:42   *they never stopped teaching and proclaiming the Good News that Jesus is the Christ.*

   You know that I have not hesitated to preach anything that would be

Acts 20:20   *helpful to you, but have taught you publicly and* _____

_____

If you are in a group, after you have done this, talk together about what you discover about friendship from this exercise. When you have finished, put the video on again.

Take a few minutes now to write down the names of each person you know personally who is not a Christian (yet!) and fits each category.

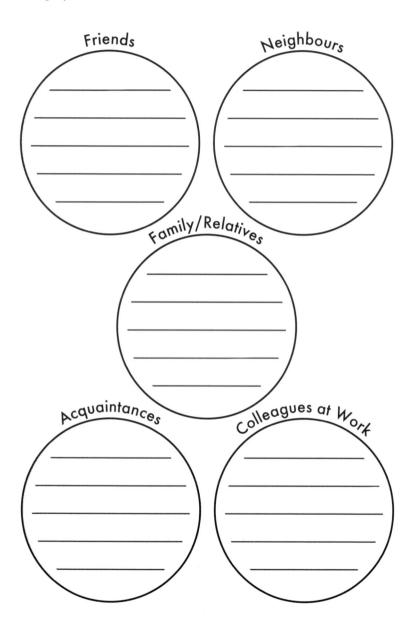

Friends

Neighbours

Family/Relatives

Acquaintances

Colleagues at Work

Now (in twos if you are in a group) offer these names which represent people whom God created and loves, to him. Pray that in the weeks and months ahead, the Spirit will do things in you to enable you to speak to these people about the Good News.

Here is a short Bible study that you can do, whether you are in a group or on your own. If you are in a group, spend some time discussing together your discoveries. The idea of this Bible study is to look at how our lives can be models for others. The idea of this exercise is not to condemn us! But we should be challenged, and made to think of our responsibility of representing Jesus and his standards to a world that has fallen so far away from them.

Philippians 2:14–15

- We are God's children living in a fallen world. What kind of lives should we lead?

Mathew 5:14–16

- What kind of things make us shine like lights in a darkened world?

1 Peter 3:1–2

- In the early church, what did the Apostle Peter teach Christian wives to do in order to win their unbelieving husbands? (There's enough to think about in the first two verses!)

Read 2 Corinthians 9:6–15 and Mark 4:26–29.

The Corinthian passage has often been used to encourage financial giving. But it should also be applied to evangelism. We give out the Good News, sharing the fruit of the Spirit. The key is to sow generously.

DAILY STUDY

- Pray regularly this week, and from now on, for the names you wrote down on p30. You might want to take a different category each day – see how the Holy Spirit directs you.
- See if you can invite one or more round for a meal or a coffee, or go out for a drink at the pub etc. Don't set them up – *'What kind of quiche do you like, and by the way what do you think of God!'* – You are building up a friendship which God can use to reveal his love.
- When it comes round to Christmas, have a party. Invite a few neighbours from each side of your house, and a few from across the road. Be normal and don't ram the gospel down their throats! Invite them to come to your carol service and give them a copy of my booklet, 'What's the point of Christmas'.

DAY ONE

Read Matthew 5:13–16.

Salt has certain characteristics that we are encouraged to exhibit.

- **Salt purifies**. It cleanses and prevents the spreading of infection and corruption.
- **Salt heals**. We live in a wounded world that needs healing.
- **Salt preserves**. It preserves from decay. It preserves good and promotes life.

- **Salt adds flavour**. It adds taste to life. (Note: If too much salt is used it can spoil the flavour of food!)
- **Salt creates thirst**. It stirs a craving deep down inside .

Reflect on these characteristics of salt and pray them into your life and situation.

Prayer

Loving Father,
Lead us by your Spirit to witness to our faith in Christ.
May what we do build up the fellowship of his Church.
May how we live speak of his word to the world.
May what we say testify to our life in him.
So that, as we know and love him more,
others may come to know and love him too... Amen.

DAY TWO

Effective healthy growth of the Church is contingent upon four main characteristics in its outreach.

Acts 2:47
- **Continuous**. The church of Acts grew every day.
  Evangelism should be continuous. It goes on all the time.

John 20:21
- **Congregational**. Jesus sends each one of us and gives the Holy Spirit to help us.
  Evangelism should be congregational. The whole Church mobilised.

I Thessalonians 2:7–8
- **Caring**. Paul showed great care and gentleness.
  Evangelism should be caring, demonstrated by love and sensitivity to people's needs.

Colossians 1:28–29
- **Conserving**. Paul's desire was to see Christians grow into maturity.
  Evangelism should be conserving. It is our desire that each new believer grows spiritually and becomes active in the life of the Church.

Pray that evangelism will be continuous, congregational, caring and conserving.

Prayer

For evangelism in your church:

Father, bless the church today in its evangelism. Help us never to give up in the spreading of your word; may each person in the church be inspired and equipped to evangelise; send us the Holy Spirit that we may love as you loved, and help us to ensure that all those who give their lives to you find a secure place in your family to serve you faithfully, through Jesus Christ our Lord... Amen

Read Luke 6:46–49

In this well known passage, Jesus makes clear that it is the wise person who builds on the rock of the word of God. During this course you have been hearing a lot about friendship evangelism.

Spend a few moments today listening quietly to what God is saying to you in all of this. How does he want to use you in friendship evangelism?

Think about the names you wrote down in Exercise Two, p30. During this time of quiet see if there are any names that the Lord particularly underlines.

Remembering the story you read earlier, be wise and build today on the word God has given you!

Spend some time in prayer for your non-Christian friends and contacts.

Prayer

Dear Lord,

Thank you for all the friends who have encouraged me in my faith, and in whom I have seen the light of Jesus.

Thank you that your word makes it clear that Christ lives in me and he wishes to reveal himself through me to my friends, through how I live and through what I speak.

Please forgive me for the times I have failed to honour you in my words and in my life, and give me boldness and love to share my faith with others who have yet to find you.

Through Jesus Christ my Lord… Amen

DAY FOUR

A bachelor psychiatrist travelled around giving a lecture entitled *Ten Commandments for Parents*. Then he married and he and his wife had their first child. He changed the title of his lecture to *Ten Suggestions for Parents*. In due course the second child arrived and he changed the title again to *Ten Hints for Parents*. When the third child came along he quit lecturing!

Spend some time today considering and praying for your own family: parents, brothers, sisters, partners and children.

First, take a look at a number of verses from a variety of books from the Bible: Exodus 20:12; Psalm 90:16; Romans 12:9–19; Ephesians 4:32.

Take these Bible truths to pray for yourself and your family.

Prayer

Dear Lord, please give us the grace to have your strength and enabling power in fulfilling our God-given roles in the family, and from this day to build a family relationship that will be honouring to Christ and a living testimony to those who are unbelievers. Amen

DAY FIVE

Read Philippians 1:1–30.

The Apostle Paul could so easily have been discouraged about his circumstances. God has used him widely, and now he is in chains and confined in prison in Rome. Whether he will die or not he does not know, but if death does come he will rejoice in the presence of Christ. If he remains, he will continue to serve God as best he can. And continue to serve God he did! He was inspired to write some letters like Ephesians, Philippians, Colossians and Philemon. And the guards became his mission field.

Q. Was Paul restricted?   **A.** Yes

Q. Was Paul limited?   **A.** Yes

Q. Was Paul surrounded by opportunities?   **A.** Yes

1 Corinthians 4:16

The Apostle Paul's attitude and example should humble us and encourage us to imitate him.

What are your circumstances? Are they difficult or easy? If they are difficult, remember Paul, who even in prison still evangelised. Whatever your situation, pray that the Spirit will give you boldness to use the opportunities given for sharing the Good News.

Prayer

And this is my prayer, that your love may abound more and more in knowledge and depth of insight, so that you may be able to discern what is best and may be pure and blameless until the day of Christ, filled with the fruit of righteousness that comes through Jesus Christ – to the glory and praise of God.

Philippians 1:9–11

DAY SIX

The word **ministry** comes from the Greek word 'diakonos' meaning 'one who serves'. The word **laity** comes from the Greek word 'Laos' meaning 'the people of God'.

Read again 1 Corinthians 12:12–30.

The Apostle emphasises that it is the body which is given gifts for ministry, not just selected parts. Pray that we may learn to be servants and continue to serve faithfully. (God has called us to be faithful, not successful!)

Prayer

Consider the following prayer from Evelyn Underhill and then, resting with 'The Good Shepherd', spend time talking to him and listening to him about this course.

We offer ourselves, one way or another, to try to work for God. We want, as it were, to be among the sheepdogs employed by the Good Shepherd. Have you ever watched a good sheepdog at work? He is not an emotional animal. He goes on with his job quite steadily; takes no notice of bad weather, rough ground, or his own comfort. He seldom or never stops to be stroked. Yet his faithfulness and intimate communion with his master are one of the loveliest things in the world. Now and then he looks at the shepherd. And when the time comes for rest, they are generally to be found together. Let this be the model of your love... Amen

Evelyn Underhill

PS: Don't forget to keep praying for those friends!

Answers to Exercise One:

1 his brother Simon, 2 Nathaniel, 3 her neighbours, 4 his ex-colleagues,
5 his family

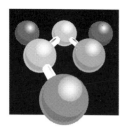

SESSION 4
How can I share my story?

STORIES ARE IMPORTANT

Jesus used parables as one of the most effective ways of communicating truth. People love hearing stories, and we have a great story to tell them!

The Gospel message needs to be communicated in three parts:

- **His story**. God's story from Genesis through to the life, death and resurrection of Jesus
- **Your story**. Which tells of God coming in power into your life and what that has meant to you
- **Their story**. How God's story relates to the person you are witnessing to.

A CLEAR STORY

In this session we shall concentrate on your story.

Come and listen, all you who fear God,
let me tell you what he has done for me.

Psalm 66:16

John 9:25

One thing I do know: I was blind, but now I can see.

Acts 4:20

For we cannot help speaking about what we have seen and heard.

In these verses we find several people who have met with God and love to tell others the story of what has happened. We are all called to be a witness to Jesus.

There is a difference between a witness and a lawyer: a witness simply tells the court what he has experienced; the lawyer has to plead the case. An evangelist is like the lawyer – not all of us are called to be this; but we are all called to give an account of what we have seen, heard and experienced of God.

We have a great story to tell, but we must make sure we have the story straight, so that others can understand us. We also need to listen carefully to their particular need, so that we can relate the right part of the story to meet that need.

DIFFERENT KINDS OF STORIES

There are four parts to our personal story:

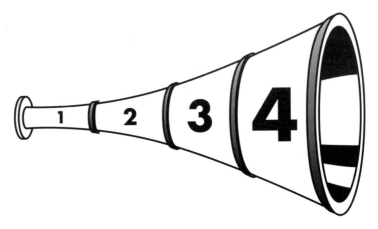

PART 1
My life before I was a Christian

We don't need a conversion date to prove we are Christians. Whichever way your conversion happened, you should give some thought to what your life was like before. What were your attitudes, behaviour and feelings about life like?

PART 2
How I realised I needed Jesus Christ

What made you turn to Christ? What particular need did you have which Jesus met? The kind of things that come to mind are truth, forgiveness, healing, hope, eternal life. We need to emphasise that this was the meeting of a person, not the taking on of a doctrine.

PART 3
How I committed my life to Jesus Christ

Where and how did you enter into a relationship with Jesus? Was it sudden or gradual? What exactly did you do to become a committed Christian?

PART 4
What it means to me now

What difference has it made to you becoming a Christian? What are the benefits? What has been the cost? From your experience, why would you encourage others to turn to Christ?

When you share your story, you will probably only share one or two parts at a time.

Guidelines in preparing your story

- Pray.

James 1:5

If any of you lacks wisdom, he should ask God who gives generously to all.

- Write it out.

1 Peter 3:15

Always be prepared to give an answer to everyone who asks you
Don't write pages – make it short, so that you can remember it easily.

- Be gentle and respect the person you are talking to.

1 Peter 3:15

But do this with gentleness and respect.

- Be honest and don't exaggerate. Share your struggles, and show you are human, but also show that you have a God who understands our weaknesses and difficulties.

- Avoid negative remarks about other religions and other denominations. We do not need to put other religions down to lift Jesus up.

- Make use of Bible references.

Hebrews 4:12

For the word is living and active, sharper than any two-edged sword.
But don't Bible bash!

- Don't use religious clichés.

1 Corinthians 2:1
(Jerusalem Bible)

As for me, my brothers, when I came to you it was not with any show or oratory or philosophy, but simply to tell you what God had guaranteed.
Note: the word, 'simply'!

- Keep it short and to the point.

For group leaders

Before you start the video, find out how people have progressed with the Daily Studies. Has anyone made any plans to have neighbours round to their home? Encourage the faint-hearted!

Tonight the group members will be putting together their story which they can use for witnessing. Make sure you give plenty of time for Exercise Two. You will need to be a time-keeper for the exercises. Take a look through them before the start of the evening and work out how much time you want to allow. Try to encourage people to write in the space given so they can keep their answers short. When they tell their story to each other, encourage them to be honest with each other about how the story sounds. If, for example, the person telling the story is using a lot of clichés, it is important that this is challenged – gently, of course!

EXERCISE ONE

You have heard on the video a number of people give answers to these questions. Now you carry on, filling in the remaining blank spaces with other problems you are aware of, and placing in the next column the solutions that Jesus offers to the problems. For those in groups, do this exercise in twos and threes and work on it together.

Common problems	what Jesus Christ offers
Loneliness	Friendship, love.
Fear	Love. 'Perfect love casts out fear'
_____	_____
_____	_____
_____	_____
_____	_____
_____	_____
_____	_____

Think of the people you know who have yet to meet Jesus. What are their problems? How could you share with them the solutions Jesus offers.

• Name	Ideas on presentation
eg. Sylvia	Tell her about Gods peace.
_____	_____
_____	_____
_____	_____
_____	_____

Pray together in your twos and threes for your unbelieving friends who have come to mind during this exercise. Pray particularly that you would be given opportunity to speak to them this week.

EXERCISE TWO

Fill in the following four sections. Make it fairly brief at this stage, (5mins) you can use more time during the week for working on it further. Use the questions to help you complete each part.

PART 1 – My life before I was a Christian

What problems or difficult situations were you facing?

_____

_____

_____

Prayer

O make me understand it, help me to take it in.
What it meant to thee, the Holy One, to bear away my sin… Amen.

DAY FOUR

Acts 7:54–58

Stephen was a martyr who laid down his life for the glory of God. Read Acts 7:54 to 8:1.

There are two sides to Stephen's death: on the one hand 7:54 and on the other 7:55–56. Stephen's death introduces us to the figure who is going to dominate the rest of the book of Acts (v58). This Saul was Saul of Tarsus who was to become Paul, the Apostle to the Gentiles.

Stephen dies after just one sermon. Was his life prematurely cut off and untimely thrown away? **No!** His life was the fuel which set alight a flame for the glory of God in the ancient world that has no parallel!

If we had been Stephen, having delivered such a powerful sermon, we might have liked to see at least a few people fall to their knees and become Christians. But apparently there were no conversions – Stephen could have been quite dejected. But he wasn't because his peace came from being obedient to his Master rather than from seeing results.

Much of our evangelism will seem unproductive. We will explain the gospel, tell our story, sense the power of the Spirit, and there might seem to be little evidence of the person being touched by God. But, like Stephen, we will need to develop that discipline of faithfully sowing the seed of God's word in the power of the Spirit and leaving the results to God. Who knows what Saul of Tarsus might be nearby listening to your conversation?

Prayer

Heavenly Father, thank you for the example of Stephen who humbled himself to wait at tables, yet who was also given such a wonderful vision of your glory.
Grant me that same grace, to so love you and your word and, being empowered by your Spirit, may I be freely available to you as a messenger of your word.
Please use me today to share the Good News of your Son with someone who has yet to meet him… Amen.

Spend some time praying for those unbelieving friends whose names you have written down on p30. Listen to the Spirit – is he calling you to speak to any of them? Perhaps he might reveal a particular need that one of them has, that God desires to meet. Be open to the Spirit's promptings today.

Read Acts 13:1–3.

It was while the Church at Antioch was worshipping and fasting that the Holy Spirit said,

Set apart for me Barnabas and Saul for the work to which I have called them.

Worship and evangelism are bound together. The reason for this is because worship is giving glory to God. So if we are worshipping God and desiring his glory, can we be unmoved by the fact that there are areas of our country and world where God is not being glorified? That is one reason why worship and evangelism go together. In worship and evangelism, God is glorified.

In the last century, Henry Martyn, a Cambridge scholar, turned his back on academic glory to go to India. In India he watched people bowing and prostrating before pagan images and he heard someone tell of a vision they had of Jesus bowing before Mahomet. Henry Martyn wrote:

I was cut to the soul at this blasphemy. I could not endure existence if Jesus was not glorified; it would be hell to me if he were thus dishonoured.

Today, many in the church have lost this deeply felt emotion for the glory of God.

Spend some time now in worship, and as you glorify God allow your heart to be moved for the lost. Ask the Holy Spirit to pray through you for the world. As the Spirit stirs in you in worship and intercessory prayer for the lost in the world, you may well begin to feel some of the deep places in the heart of God.

Romans 8:26   *We do not know what we ought to pray, but the Spirit himself intercedes for us with groans that words cannot express.*

Prayer

Say this prayer slowly line by line. Allow the Spirit to move in you.

Come, Holy Spirit.
Come and move in my heart.
Come and pray through me for the lost.
Come and give me again a vision of the glory of God.
Stir in me a longing to see God glorified.
Father, Son and Holy Spirit I worship you.
Holy is your name… Amen

DAY SIX

Read Acts 16:6–10

The Apostles found themselves being sent not so much to people they had chosen, as to people God had chosen for them.

Time and time again their own inclinations were corrected either by direct divine intervention or by God-created circumstances.

Acts 16:6–8   In Acts 16, Paul and his team experience frustration after frustration. Doors were closing against them rather than opening, frustrating their plans rather than fulfilling them. They had to learn to die to their own plans for the sake of God's plans; to die to their own timetable in order to live by God's.

Have you experienced frustration in trying to share the Good News in places where you thought it was obvious to share it? Perhaps God has been closing some doors, in order to channel you in the right direction.

Spend some time asking the Lord to show you where the right mission field is.

Listen to the promptings of the Spirit

Can you sense 'a man from Macedonia' calling you? Is God showing you someone who is longing to hear the Good News, who needs you to go to them? If you do feel God is directing you to someone, then pray that the way will be made clear for you to meet with them today or at least very soon.

Prayer

Father, I abandon myself into your hands.
Do with me what you will.
Whatever you may do, I thank you.
I am ready for all, I accept all.
Charles de Foucauld   *Let only your will be done in me… Amen*

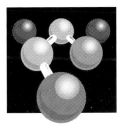

SESSION 5
How do social concern and evangelism go together?

SOCIAL JUSTICE

Social justice should be a natural part of our evangelism. It can go before evangelism, in the sense that it can open closed doors, break down prejudice, and be a bridge across which the gospel may pass. We can move from people's 'felt needs' to their 'spiritual needs'. But even if no bridge were created, God's people would still have a concern for social justice.

One of the reasons why Christ gave himself for us was

Titus 2:14 *to purify for himself a people of his own, eager to do what is good.*

Part of these good deeds is to struggle against everything that condemns people to a sub-human existence: hunger, disease, poverty, inequality and injustice.

Positive programmes designed to better the conditions of the disadvantaged and neglected are indispensable parts of evangelism and should have the full support of the church.

The poor – Biblical perspectives

The Old Testament uses several different Hebrew words when referring to the poor:

Ani is the most common word, used 77 times. It literally means 'a person bowed down'. 'Ani' is contrasted not with the rich, but with the oppressor.

Anaw is used 18 times, and refers to people who feel they have little value before God.

Ebyon is used 60 times and refers to 'beggars'.

All these words are full of emotion, and call for urgent change.

In the New Testament, we find many references to the social conditions of the time. There is talk of landowners, tax collectors, labourers, slaves, honest and dishonest stewards, creditors, unjust judges and widows pleading for their rights. Such references bring to light extremes of wealth and poverty, power and powerlessness.

The most common New Testament Greek word for poor is **ptochos** which literally means to 'duck away in fear'. There are other words: the lowly, the needy, the insignificant, the weak and the oppressed.

Philippians 2:7 *God has shown his solidarity with the poor and powerless by sending his Son who took upon himself the form of a servant.*

'Justice' is the opposite of 'Just us'. God's good gifts are not for just us.

EVANGELISM AND SOCIAL ACTION

We cannot separate evangelism, signs and wonders and social action. There is no competition between lighthouse keepers and lifeboat savers.

Mother Theresa once said,

We try to pray through our work by doing it with Jesus, for Jesus, to Jesus. That helps us to put our whole heart and soul into doing it. The dying, the crippled, the mentally ill, the unwanted, the unloved - they are Jesus in disguise.

For group leaders

Before starting the video find out how people have progressed with the Daily Studies. You may want to spend some time encouraging people to share some of the answers they have found to the first piece of homework (objections to the Christian faith). But be disciplined – this could take all night! Make it a sharing of ideas and thoughts, rather than a full scale discussion. Of course, there are no quick and easy answers to these questions, but there are clues, and group members will have discovered some of these.

Work out the timings for this evening. Exercise Two is particularly important, so make sure you leave enough time for it.

Following Exercise Three, you may want to make a note of what you feel the Lord is saying to your group and pass it on to the church leadership, who can discern what God is saying to the church about ministry to the poor.

EXERCISE ONE

We hear a great deal about 'the poor'. Jesus said,

Luke 6:20 *Blessed are you who are poor*

What do we mean when we speak of 'the poor'. Who are they? Where are they? What immediately springs to your mind?

Read Deuteronomy 15:4–5; 7–11.

For those in groups, talk together about this passage. After your discussion, be silent and reflect for a few moments before closing this discussion with the following prayer:

Then ask the Lord if there is other fruit he wants you to bear. Is God calling you to bear fruit through some kind of social action?

We are confronted with insurmountable opportunities.

Pray for God's eyes to see what we can pray and do this day for a relative, a friend or an enemy.

Prayer

Grant that we may walk as Christ walked;
Grant that what the Spirit was in him,
such he may be also in us;
Grant that our lives may be re-fashioned
after the pattern of his life;
Grant that we may do today here on earth
what Christ would have done, and in the
way he would have done it;
Grant that we may become vessels of his grace,
instruments of his will –
To thy honour and glory;
JH Jowett   *Through Jesus Christ our Lord... Amen.*

DAY SIX

Read Psalm 46:10 James 1:19.

Sometimes, somewhere we know that without silence words lose their meaning, that without listening speaking no longer heals, that without
Henri Nouwen   *closeness distance cannot cure.*

Spend some time today being still, being reflective over this session on social concern and pray that the Lord may distil all that you have seen, heard, thought, and responded to. Pray for grace and strength to apply the distilled drops of wisdom.

Prayer

Lord, our heavenly Father, whose Son came not to be served but to serve, bless us in our desire and commitment to serve you and others in this world. Give us wisdom, patience and courage to strengthen the weak and raise up those who fall, that being inspired by your love we may minister in your name by word and deed to the suffering, the friendless and the needy; for the sake of your Son, who laid down his life for us, Jesus Christ our Saviour... Amen.

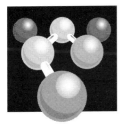

SESSION 6
How can we receive power for evangelism?

PENTECOST

The word **Pentecost** literally means '50th'. It was the 50th day after the Passover. In Acts, Pentecost falls 50 days after the Great Passover of the Cross and Resurrection. We cannot understand the significance of Pentecost without the Cross.

On the day of Pentecost, Peter says

Acts 2:38

Repent and be baptised every one of you in the name of Jesus Christ for the forgiveness of your sins. And you will receive the gift of the Holy Spirit.

Pentecost fulfills the promise of Jesus:

Acts 1:8

You will receive power when the Holy Spirit comes on you.

Pentecost is a missionary event. This festival was also called the Feast of the First Fruits, and in Acts 2 we see the first fruits of the harvest of the gospel.

A direct result of the Holy Spirit is evangelism. When the Spirit came at Pentecost, the disciples became *Saints in Evangelism!*

The Spirit is the moving power, energy, and inspiration behind **all** evangelism.

THE NEED

1 Three types of missionaries

There are three types of missionaries in Acts 8, 11 & 13:

Acts 8:1
* the stay-put missionaries like the Apostles who stayed put in Jerusalem

Acts 8:4
* the share-as-you-go missionaries like Philip

Acts 13:2
* the set apart missionaries like Barnabas and Saul.

We need all three types of missionary in the church today.

THE HOLY SPIRIT

2 In prayer

The Holy Spirit inspires prayer and his power is released through prayer. The New Testament knows no evangelism without prayer. The first thing the disciples do after the Ascension of Jesus is to pray and they are seldom far from a prayer meeting.

Acts 1:14

We are instructed to pray:

Matthew 9:37–38
* for workers to be sent to the mission field

Acts 13:1–3
* for guidance – who to send and where

Ephesians 6:19–20
* for the success of the message

- for protection and help for all in evangelism
- for those who make themselves enemies to the gospel.

3 In personal evangelism

In Acts, God directs Philip using an angel and promptings of the Spirit.

Acts 8:26–40

The gift of the word of knowledge can be used.

4 In church evangelism

In their missionary travels in Asia Minor, Paul and his companions are directed where to go, and even shown where they must not go. Through a wonderful dream, they are directed to go to Macedonia and God opens up an amazing new door into Europe.

Acts 16:1–15

5 Witnessing with words and deeds

When Jesus sent out his first mission teams, he gave them power and authority to drive out all demons and to cure diseases, and he sent them to preach the Kingdom of God and to heal the sick.

Luke 9:1–6

Acts 3:1–10
Acts 19:11–16

It was therefore natural for the disciples to continue this kind of evangelism.

6 Spiritual warfare

The Holy Spirit helps us to see things as God sees them, and therefore helps us see what is going on in the heavenly places. When we engage in evangelism we engage in spiritual warfare because Satan will always be opposed to the gospel being spread.

2 Corinthians 4:4

Paul tells us that Satan has blinded the mind of the unbeliever, which means every act of personal evangelism will involve spiritual warfare.

1 Thessalonians 2:18

There were times when even Paul's missionary plans were frustrated by Satan, so we should not be surprised if we meet resistance.

CONCLUSION

We all need to be filled with the Spirit if we are to be *Saints in Evangelism*. We need the Spirit:

- to inspire our prayer
- for direction in personal and church evangelism
- for witnessing with signs and wonders
- for spiritual warfare.

We need to have the gift of the Holy Spirit to move powerfully in us individually and as churches if we are to be effective in evangelism, so that the Holy Spirit can reveal Jesus through us to the world.

EXERCISE

EXERCISE

For group leaders

This is the last meeting of the group, and one of the things you will need to establish at some point is what happens next. You may find it useful to meet once again next week to tie up any loose ends. The Study Guide Daily Studies will carry on for another week.

As you meet, check out how people progressed with their Daily Studies. Has anyone invited 'Mrs Smith' to lunch yet?

Are there any other plans or projects that the group or the church needs to consider in connection with social concern?

There are three exercises in this session, and again it will be important to go through and check how long you want the group to spend on each one. The last one is clearly crucial, and it is important that every member of the group receives ministry for a release of the Spirit for evangelism.

During the course you may well have collected many ideas and suggestions for developing friendship evangelism in the church. Why not make this into the form of a report and hand it in to your church leadership for their consideration?

EXERCISE ONE

Take a moment to reflect on your church and personal prayer life. Can any changes and improvements be made to develop prayer in relation to evangelism? For those in groups, discuss this together.

EXERCISE TWO

Think about the area your church serves.

Where has the gospel been well received (socially and geographically)?

Where are the barren places?

After thinking and talking about this, spend some time listening to the Lord and see if you sense the Spirit of God directing the church to evangelise a particular region or section of your community. If you have a strong sense of God speaking about a particular area, drop a note to your church leadership who can look at this alongside notes from others doing this course.

End this exercise by praying for the barren places that you have discussed.

EXERCISE THREE

This is the last exercise of the course!

As on the video, form groups of three to pray for and minister to one another (two ministering to one, taking it in turns to change role). Ask that the Holy Spirit would come on each person with power and boldness for evangelism. If you are not sure what to pray, here is a prayer you could use which is based on Acts 4:29–30.

Say with the laying on of hands:

Father in heaven,
thank you that you have given us the wonderful gift of your Holy Spirit. Send now your Spirit on _____.
Enable her/him to speak your word with great boldness.
Stretch out your hand to work through her/him signs and wonders in the name of your holy servant Jesus, that many may experience your power and your love through her/his witness.

Remain quiet for a while, allowing the Spirit to work. Make use of the gift of tongues if you have it. Ask God to give you prophetic words and pictures to encourage the person you are praying for. Open your heart in faith, believing that God is working powerfully in this person's life.

If you are on your own, pray for the Spirit to fill and empower you and use the above prayer for yourself.

DAILY STUDY

DAY ONE

Read Acts 1:14, 2:42 and 6:1–7.

In Acts 1 the Apostles, Mary the mother of Jesus and others devoted themselves to prayer.
In Acts 2 the 3,000 new Christians devoted themselves to the Apostles' teaching, fellowship, breaking of bread and prayer.
In Acts 6 the Apostles devoted themselves to prayer and the ministry of the word.

The word **devoted** means 'intensely enthusiastic, ardent, dedicated and consecrated'. Pray today that the Holy Spirit will help your will to be devoted and dedicated to have communion with the Lord.

JC Ryle

Fear not because your prayer is stammering, your words feeble and your language poor. Jesus can understand you.

CH Spurgeon

When we pray, the simpler our prayers are the better; the plainest, humblest language which expresses our meaning is best.

Prayer

Thank God for the ministry you received in the group and pray that God will continue to fill you with his Spirit for evangelism.

Read Acts 4:23–31.

Peter and John have just been interrogated by a group of very powerful and distinguished Jewish leaders. Most people would be greatly intimidated by this, but John and Peter both find that in that situation they are given great boldness and wisdom. On return, despite knowing the storm clouds are gathering, they pray for a further release of the Spirit.

Take a look at this prayer.
What do you learn about prayer from it?
Where do you think God wants you to speak for him with boldness?
Ask him about this today.

Think again about the people whose names you wrote down on p30.
Could there be an opportunity to speak boldly to any of these today?
Pray for them again.

Prayer

Father, I am weak, but you are strong.
I have no words, but you sent your Son who is the Word.
I have no love, but you sent your Spirit who pours your love into our hearts.
Come touch me today:
fill me afresh with the life-giving Spirit
and use me today in compassion and boldness
to tell others about your Son, Jesus,
that the rivers of life may flow from my heart to others... Amen.

DAY THREE

Read Ephesians 5:15–20.

What does it mean to be filled with the Holy Spirit? Simply, it means being like Jesus. When I'm filled with the Holy Spirit, the risen Christ in all of his mighty powerful presence lives in my body, thinks with my mind, loves with my heart, speaks with my lips. And since he came to seek and save the lost, he walks around in my body, seeking and saving the lost.

John 15:7   Being filled with the Holy Spirit means, according to John, to abide in Christ. That is what the Christian life is all about – walking day by day in the fullness and joy and the power and adventure of the third person of the Trinity, God the Holy Spirit. As a result, God the Son will be exalted and honoured and worshipped and praised and adored. That is the role of the Holy

Spirit. He did not come to glorify himself.

Pray that we may discover a fresh experience of being filled with the Spirit today, so that Jesus will be glorified.

Prayer

Give us now, O merciful Father, thy Holy Spirit,
that we may be strengthened for the work of this
day, through Jesus Christ thy Son, our Lord… Amen.

DAY FOUR

Read 1 Corinthians 13.

This is probably one of the most famous passages in the Bible. Try to imagine that you are reading this passage for the first time, and allow God to speak to you through it.

God is love, so you could substitute 'God' for 'love' in v4–7 which gives you an insight into the character of God.

John 3:16 *God so loved the world that he gave his only Son, Jesus Christ, to save us from our sins and to give us eternal life.*

God's love is expressed towards the lost world, and such is the extent of his love that he sends his beloved Son to rescue us.

Let the Spirit explore your heart today.

Are there any hard places that need softening?
Is there any forgiving that needs to be done?
Give some thought to your relationship with your unbelieving friends, especially those you have on your list on p30.
To what extent do you love them?

Do you love them sufficiently to be concerned for their spiritual well being now, and their eternal destiny?

Evangelism without love will be cold and clinical. But where your heart is alight with the fire of God for a person, then the Spirit of God can stir and set light to that person's life. Pray for the Spirit to come and stir up love in your heart again.

Meditate on this verse

Romans 5:5 *God has poured out his love into our hearts by the Holy Spirit whom he has given us.*

Prayer

Use the personalised version of the verse from Romans as a repetitive prayer, saying it once, then pausing and repeating it. As you do this be aware of the Spirit of God filling you with God's love. Repeat this several times until you sense God's filling is complete.

Lord God, pour your love into my heart through the Holy Spirit whom you have given me…

Now, with the love of God in your heart, pray for those on your list.

DAY FIVE

Read Matthew 24:1–14.

God has a master plan for this universe,

Acts 1:7 *The times and dates the Father has set by his own authority.*

Christ is coming again – he said so himself:

John 14:2–3 *In my Father's house are many rooms, if it were not so, I would have told you. I am going there to prepare a place for you. And if I go and prepare a place for you, I will come back and take you to be with me that you also may be where I am.*

Read Matthew 26:63–64.

What is the purpose of his Second Coming?
The Bible tells us:

Acts 17:31; 2 Timothy 4:l
1 Corinthians 15:24–28
Revelation 11:15

- Christ is coming to judge.
- Christ is coming to reign.

Until he comes

When we participate in the rich symbolism of the Lord's Supper, we have before us our motivation, our message and our marching orders. It is a missionary meal.

In the broken bread and poured-out wine, we have a powerful reminder of the price God paid for our liberation from the power and penalty of sin, and a compelling reason why we must now be totally dedicated to him and his service.

He died for all, that those who live should no longer live for themselves but for him who died for them and was raised again.

Pray that God would give you such a vision of the second coming that you will gladly labour in the harvest field until he comes.

Therefore, my dear brothers, stand firm. Let nothing move you. Always give yourselves fully to the work of the Lord, because you know that your labour in the Lord is not in vain.

Prayer

Lord, the task is not finished, keep me pressing forward, help me to be a faithful servant and witness of yours till we meet in glory… Amen.

DAY SIX

This is the last daily reading of *Saints in Evangelism*. Look back today over the six weeks during which you have been doing this course. Take a look through this Study Guide and your notes.

- What were the parts which meant a lot to you and which you will treasure?
- In what ways, if at all, has your approach to evangelism changed during this course?
- Which passage from the Bible meant most to you as you did this course? Turn it up again and read it now.

2 Corinthians 5:15

Now take a few moments to complete the following sentence which will be your commitment to ongoing friendship evangelism. This is between you and the Lord, so take a moment to think and pray about it, then complete it:

Following this course I intend to

_____

_____

1 Corinthians 15:58

Take a look at this and pray about it.

Finally, pray for your friends and neighbours whose names are on p30, and work out how you are going to continue to pray for them and evangelise them in the weeks to come.

You might like to try the Singapore '5-3-1' method, which is:

- Prayerfully seek the Lord for 5 friends who have yet to meet Christ (select from your list) and commit yourself to praying for them regularly for a year
- Ask God that by the end of the year you will have had the opportunity to speak to at least 3 of them about Christ
- Pray that by the end of the year at least 1 of them has come to Christ.

If everyone were to successfully do this, then every church would double its size every year!

Final Prayer

Heavenly Father, thank you for sending your Son, Jesus Christ into the world to save sinners.

Thank you for sending us your Holy Spirit to empower us to tell others about Christ.

Thank you for all that I have learned in this course.

Now send me out in the power of the Spirit, that I may live out all that I have learned.

Bless all who have been on this course with me and may we all live and work as Saints in Evangelism.

In the name of Jesus Christ our Lord... Amen.